The Ramblings of One Person

Happy Vith

BookLeaf Publishing

Presentation by *BookLeaf Publishing*

Web: www.bookleafpub.com

E-mail: info@bookleafpub.com

ISBN: 9789357441728

First edition 2023

PREFACE

I've come to discover that I do not care if this poetry is bad. It is just practice. I can ramble for twenty some pages and not make any sense. At least I will have slowed down and thought more carefully than I have in recent memory. I think I will be a better person at the end of this book. Or I will at least have learned to pay closer attention to the world around me and inside of me.

When I don't want to write about myself

I write about my consciousness in another place
as if that moment can be a bridge to here and now
if only in a puzzling sort of way
    full of half truths and misdiagnoses
when did I get so serious and stressed out
    nothing means anything
and a definition all depends on the stressors of a word

I guess that applies to people as well

Silence

I sometimes feel like sitting in silence
would make my thoughts return
Which is exactly what I want.
But if that's true,
why is it so hard
to stop the record from playing?

Words

I cannot think of my own
mind cluttered and stuffed with outside voices
                    but how I itch
to write words that will float around the heads of others
like swansongs in the air

Perhaps Life is Easier

when we think of ourselves as aliens
or as animals
humanity is really just a front full of pretentious ideology
but happiness is easier when it's abstract
like the sound of a tiny hard noodle going down a metal drain

When Cigarettes and Other Drugs are not Enough

I sit alone picking at skin and ruining red lipstick
when I do not know what to say
I pick up a pen
hoping that some idea will be plucked out from the pile
and stay long enough to be in conversation

How can I write poetry when I can't remember how I feel
my emotions are on the other end of the solar system
and my gravity is not strong enough to pull them back

I replace them with shitty beats I make on my computer
They bring me to the stars
        or they bring me to a grave and hand me a shovel

It really is a sad sort of happy

Out in the Water

I am alligator food
a dead bog body
slimy and slick
bloated with my own
thoughts floating like bearded moss
in that mucky, murky soup

I'm waiting five days
for that sweet release of alligator teeth

How do I start to Learn?

The hardest thing about growing up in a home
that wasn't particularly loving
is reaching a certain age and realizing
if you want to be properly loved
you have to do it yourself

but no one has ever taught you how

Seeking Genuine Connection

You keep trying to buy my love
but the currency you have is not enough
quite too literal
not enough on the spiritual
side I glide
away from you ever so slightly
like planets losing their gravitational pull
on each other

The Point

sometimes I think about the message I want to
leave behind
and realize
it's just the things I wish someone would tell me

I'm proud of you

A Self Portrait

For so long every step you've taken
Has been down the same paved, pre-determined road
Everyone else is running down.

It's lovely because it's simple

Everyone wants to know how you'll turn out
The world's largest ball of twine is slowly unravelling
And you're not quite sure if they'll like what's at the
end of the rope.

All your friends seem to be doing fine
and following their ambitions like a tail on a comet
And yet here you are
Dying at an average pace

But then you'll stop,
think about how you've seen the light
crashing onto the shores of some New Jersey beach
and catching on the early morning waves.

It's lovely because it's simple

I am glad I still exist.

Cauterize

We never talked
I just handed myself over
Let myself be molded,
drawn on,
in that red ink that tells us we failed.
We had a beginning and an end
But I never really thought we had a middle
Maybe we were only a match,
not quite the burning house everyone else saw
only too easy to put out

To kill a Bug

Is it wrong to kill a bug in my sink
If he can't fly out himself
and I am too scared to touch his
non flesh and bone

when will this ringing in my ears stop?

Paper Cranes

A perfect, white, paper square
Folded with neat precision,
Creating fine line and sharp edges where they weren't before.
A task so rooted in my brain, so familiar
My hands following the steps without thinking.
A mindless task.

It is only when I stop to think about what I'm doing,
That my hands stall,
My brain stutters,
Did I miss a step?
Is this wrong?

But just sitting here listening to you talk,
I can fold a thousand paper cranes,
Create an army of wonderous white birds,
And let them fly.

America's Best Skill is Fear Mongering

Dont focus on being "tough on crime"
be tough on the inequalities and rampant
disparities that create crime

the death penalty is inhuman
make prison about reform not punishment

We keep spreading hatred when we should focus
on Love

I am Ranting

There is too much unfairness in the world
I am not the root of it
My biggest sin may be allowing it to perpetuate
I want to do more
I want I want I want I want
I want to change the world
but can something too great to be encompassed fully in my eyes,
be molded by my feeble hands?
I cannot wrap up earth's sorrow
and wash it from this world
Perhaps I can enlist the hands and hearts of others
But what river we wash in will inevitably be filled with poison again
The smaller challenge might be to purify each other,
instead of changing the water cycle
Teach those that have been poisoned
that it is not our fault, but the fault of our ancestors,
drinking the spoiled creek, and showing their children where the water lies
There is no shame in being misled in ignorance
as long as you do not grow to hate the light

My giant green lawn is a sign of privilege
just like the golf course on the other side of the tree line
Capitalism
It's all bad for the environment

Like the capital we all strive for in some way is our poison,
our undoing
Humans forgot what society was about and
turned greedy selfish
We think we're the best species but can't see
how driven we are by ecological connections

Why must we have the best?
Why must we be the best?
Why is it a competition to exist?
But we claim to have surpassed survival of the fittest
Our intelligence is not what makes us unique
only allows us to be more sinister
and hopefully one day more peaceful

I am God

as much as the next person

The Book of Enoch tells us,
that having a thirst for knowledge
is a consequence of some age old sin,
and not some sort of intrinsic human trait.
And the man carries on to say
that if I do not believe in God
I will be punished with suffering
for thousands of years,
but I've heard that a sign of healthy democracy
is having no fear to protest.

Perhaps God is real
Perhaps they are an alien,
or an essence,
or some mystical being,
or the part of us that makes us feel alive

Perhaps God is not real at all

Perhaps they are just some made up
figure in a story,
that is too old at this point to just
get rid of

I do not care if you believe in God or not

I only care about you

Take care of yourself
and the world around you
I believe now
that we can help
our friends and neighbors
in a more tangible way
than god ever could

Droning

There is a certain kind of anxiety
that comes from the sound
of WASPs

Their hard little bodies
buzzing past your ear
each time you step outside

The sound only lasts
for a second before
it's swallowed by your relief

But there are certain WASPs
Who will make you live each day
consumed by the low murmur

of their rationalized hatred
Their droning a constant sound
that buries itself deep
in the nape of your neck

Will Two Tin Cans Tied with String Let Me Talk to Ghosts?

I have dealt with death before.
but yours was the most unbearable.
Every other funeral had been a gloomy event
tied to a person I hardly knew
It had been a week,
since I last saw you
now it's been months
that will turn into years

I was told once that I needed something to believe in,
That the idea of some type of god would make me
happier
I disagreed.
But today listening to my cousins weep,
I wish I didn't.
Maybe it would help lighten my despair if I knew
that you were somewhere better,
somewhere at all.

How are you?
Are things going well?
It's been better here, time helps
What's it like?
That's okay,
I wasn't expecting an answer.
Sometimes it just helps to talk out-loud.

www.ingramcontent.com/pod-product-compliance
Lightning Source LLC
Chambersburg PA
CBHW051722130826
49812CB00034B/1300
9789357441728